Praise for
The Blues Handbook

"Adrian S. Potter's *The Blues Handbook* is a phenomenal collection full of stunning imagery and great wisdom that can only come from a life of intense observation and reflection. The work exudes strength and mastery of Potter's role as poet, as witness. He is keenly aware of the fight as a person of color and as a poet, for 'society is always trying to kill my kind.' Potter speaks of weapons and battles, our constant fight between heaven and hell. He truly understands the power of the blues 'because once you become acquainted with them, you'll never shake loose from their grasp.' This is a poet writing at the highest level."

—HEATHER BUCHANAN, Publisher of Aquarius Press/Willow Books

"Adrian S. Potter's *The Blues Handbook* is exactly as stated. A gorgeous handbook that leaves the reader wrought with the time-honored question, 'How will I survive this?' Potter writes from a soul filled with self-doubt as he navigates the waters of his own mind. To read this manuscript is to want to reach a hand out and say, 'I know this pain.' These pages are a comforting weighted blanket for those weary of bones, those who don't know when the sun will shine again, and for those who want nothing more than to be seen for who they are at their core. And not just how much they managed to carry on bruised shoulders too small and tired for the world to rest upon. The book says 'I don't have to carry it all and I shouldn't have been expected to' in such a perfect way that only Adrian S. Potter could accomplish."

—FLORENCE SUSANNE-REPPERT, Editor-in-Chief of *Poetry as Promised*

"Potter genuinely understands the stripped, true, aching reality of being a human today. Like the blues he writes about, Potter's poetry is soulful, melancholic, and emotional. From his commentaries on social justice to his musical verses on faith and grief, *The Blues Handbook* takes the deepest parts of you and leaves them bare on the page."

—KYLIE HOY, *Oyster River Pages*

"*The Blues Handbook* by Adrian S. Potter is a deeply reflective and relevant poetic exploration of the human condition. Potter uses gripping and powerful language to paint a picture of a fractured society where simply existing as a person of color becomes an act of resistance. The collection references 'the blues' not only as a nod to the musical and cultural tradition but also as a metaphor for racial trauma and inherited depression. Through a sequence of letters to the blues, Potter examines the emotional weight of Black existence."

—BRITAIN POWERS, *Maverick Reviews*

The Blues Handbook

Poems

Adrian S. Potter

Thirty West
Publishing
•• ••
10 YEARS
2015-2025

ISBN 13: 979-8-9987727-0-2
Cover design by Josh Dale
Interior design by Josh Dale
Edited by Kinsey Krachinski
Author photo by Lowell Wagoner
First Edition: October 2025

Printed in the U.S.A.
For more titles and inquiries, please visit:
www.thirtywestph.com

To those who lit the matches that ignited my blues—this book is the smoke.

track list

ARS POETICA, OR WHY I DROP BOMBS AKA WRITE POEMS

to feel bewildered by the splintered sky
so I can create waves in a low tide
my melanin challenges all attempts to assimilate
because vulnerability can be sexy
to offer psalms of disappointment
amazing things are happening here in hell
legally I've been advised to say nothing
I don't know how to smile
sometimes I adhere to stereotypes in secret
I smile too much
society is always trying to kill my kind
since I know how to survive as both bully and victim
I want you to understand the origin of frustration
the topography of my soul remains treacherous
there's not enough space for unanswered prayers
the topography of my soul remains inviting
there's bourbon on my breath
so I don't hold onto nostalgia like a pocketknife
a desire to remain connected in a detached society
to pierce the bulletproof glass surrounding my heart
a noose chokes out all my unhinged lyrics
I sing in the morning like I want to forget the night

TELL THEM A STORY

without tragedy, pretend happy endings exist.
Toss worry inside a closet, nail the door shut,

and never let it escape. Don't tell them about
the evil that gets unraveled and hymned out

every Sunday morning, just to get stitched back
into the fabric of flashy clothes the next Friday

night. Tell them something vaguely comforting:
Adirondack chairs on a lakeshore, a soft breeze

nudging clouds through the flawless blue sky
Tell them the heart of a hummingbird beats

faster than its wings, even if you're not sure
that's accurate. Don't tell them about the pain

of an injured soul or how it feels to be a wishbone
pulled apart by desire and duty. Don't tell them

how lust chews its carnal claim into your hide
and spits you out whole for the world to judge.

IF LIFE IS AS GOOD AS PEOPLE CLAIM, WHY DOES IT FEEL LIKE I'M JUST WAITING FOR ITS CONCLUSION

If heaven was on earth, I would ask for all the small pleasures
I crave but never request because doing so would feel sinful.

And for that statement, I'll surely catch hell. This admission
will upset all the righteous and judgmental folks who read it.

I'm a man of complex simplicity. What I want, mainly, is a
year that won't test my patience before it ends. The ability

to choose my battles and weapons wisely. A care package
on my porch and no bills in the mailbox. More chances

to see the summer breeze slow waltz with the trees
or new grass sprout from a yard that was clearly dying.

To hear my wife say I'm sweet when I feel wicked
as this world that wants to whittle me down. You see,

like many, I was born, and things only got worse from there.
In the empty chill of a therapist's office, I sigh and confess

everything I should stop doing and get told every habit
I need to start. But none of that sounds like living to me.

I run endless miles on a treadmill some mornings, knowing
it's a frayed metaphor for my tenuous existence. When what

I most desire is to never need to worry about performance
reviews or creditors calling and to spend all my time reading,

browsing record shops, and helping others. For the people
I care about to never feel pain. To learn how to make biscuits

from scratch. For the ball in pickup basketball with the game
on the line. To receive signs from God that the mistakes I make

can eventually be made right. I'm a card-carrying member of
the self-help-becomes-self-hatred club, holding survival by

my teeth like a baby does a nipple. Living remains as basic
as listening to A Love Supreme by John Coltrane while folding

laundry that I've neglected for a week. Waking up unsure
whether I should give up or try again. Watching personal

growth gurus preach their gospel of synthetic optimism
on YouTube until I scream and wonder if manufacturing

positivity is worth all the effort. Still, there is something
about knowing what's most likely to end you that pushes

you to persist with more passion. I remain certain my demise
will be triggered by the self-sabotaging behavior, fried foods,

and dysfunctional relationships I indulge in despite knowing
better. Red meat. Red wine. Myself, whistling my discontent

in an office while heating leftovers in a breakroom microwave,
never realizing I'm squandering my future. Or my secret talent

of reducing myself to ash without burning. Here, finally, I can
envision a world worth living in, against my better judgment.

One that feels like it has direction even though all roads
lead nowhere. A world I love so much that I cannot stop

letting it kill me, slowly. So if I must live, then I will keep on
doing it recklessly while feigning that I'll never die. If I must.

BLUES NOTE NO. 1

Dear Blues,

Welcome to the album release listening party of your bite-marked soul. Play deep cuts so I can two-step to them before society's indifference makes a ghost out of you. Nobody smiles anymore, so here's my mouth, sketched as a straight line. A closed-lipped border between confession and confusion. Thumbing through your liner notes, I consider your themes. I understand your libretto like I do a river—wide and bottomless. It's the falling season again. A familiar heartbreak in my head while I tumble downward with prayers for softer ground fresh on my lips. I wish your life upon no one, born out of that which will become your undoing. Imagine, instead, becoming a bittersweet anthem to the evening, a soundtrack of soft-spoken desires, an echo of our joys as an open palm. But eventually, your fingers close, reality hits with bare-knuckled precision, and we learn to take punches and remain standing. That's you being you. That is the blues.

DANCING MACHINES

All this time, we thought we needed signed permission
slips to get down. To shake our theoretical moneymakers
or strut our proverbial stuff. Squeegee away the glistening
sweat that adorns our foreheads as we freestyle moves
for every groove. My people are talented at inventing
brand new funk in the time it takes to get on the good foot
and electric slide our backsides across the ballroom floor
of whatever function is popping tonight. Like a young
Michael Jackson, we all evolve into dancing machines,
willing slaves to nothing but the rhythm, with its pulsating
basslines and deliberate insistence on delivering joy.
No wonder we dare to imagine a world without police
brutality or prejudice. Each day we nod our heads
to the notion of harmony, singing every lovely word
off-key before this harsh world can distort our lyrics.

DEFINING THE BLUES

This poem is for those fortunate few
who have never experienced a tinge
of sorrow in their weary bones
who have avoided the marrow-deep
ache of broken hallelujahs
those blessed folks who haven't had
their ordinary lives splayed open
by accident or ill intent
this poem was written so they
might recognize the blues.

This poem is not for the desperate
masses who have flinched at the sight
of an eviction notice yet remained
poker-faced while signing bad checks
and waited for a lucky break
that never arrived
this poem is not for those men
and women who would pawn
their identities to the highest broker
those people already know
the blues all too well.

Forgive me—I am not a wise man
I do not know why deceit sometimes
tastes like honey or what pollinates
the familiar with thoughts of discontent
or whether these are truly the things
that cause forehead creases,
thinning hair, and meager hopes
but somewhere between moments
of genuine concern and caring less
the breeze of time blows through
and rearranges all that we cherish
before long, the wrong things
become sacred and solace fades
into the ether of the past
nothing good ever lasts
that's the only lesson this simpleton
can claim he can teach.

For those who have never felt the blues
try to understand they spawn
a holy longing in the night
for the bodies we reach out to,
hoping they are miraculously there
and the misery that comes
when they are not.

The blues are a deep-set stain
on the daily drudgery
of a workaholic life
while we follow the same
freedom-crushing route
our parents traveled.

The blues are what has bitterly
transformed the earth's populace
into a never-ending cacophony
of lonely souls lobbing prayers
up toward God like hand grenades.

Thus the blues continue on,
whether you're acquainted with them or not
as unexplainable as a world filled
with suicide on a full moon night
but before happiness falls out
of reach like an itch that won't die
I will dole out the remaining definitions
of the blues that I know:

When you look out in the darkness
to find nothing but a cold pillow to clutch
that is the blues
when your unresolved options get shuffled
like playing cards with consequences dealt out randomly
that is the blues
when you stay home wondering about those long gone
or those making love with someone that's not you
that is the blues.

So heed this poem as your final warning
to avoid the blues at all costs;
because once you become acquainted with them,
you'll never shake loose from their grasp.

A Partial Inventory of Personal Excuses

Blame the barroom, with its cheap hooch and dim corners. Blame familiar fables, insincere laughter, slow dances. Blame the secret door knock. Blame the splintered darkness, blue lights, licentious thoughts. Clinched fists, sucker punches, and split lips. Blame the slender-legged woman in the alley, asking strangers for a light. Blame the thigh highs and her doe-eyed offer for a nightcap. Blame the misplaced, blame the misguided. Blame broken-down Fords and poorly lit parking lots. Blame each quarrel, every wrong turn. Blame the tear-stained fractured fairytales people recite instead of facts. Blame charm bracelets and sundresses. Blame back porches and screen doors. Blame the pastoral call of the country, with its gravel roads and cautionary tales. Lip gloss and bubblegum. Failed promises and reluctant apologies. Blame the foul-mouthed. Blame the foul weathered. Blame the edges, enticing me to fall again.

NOTES TO SELF ON SELF-PRESERVATION

1. Guys who act tough have fragile egos. Also, secrets.

2. Hang around long enough and you'll eventually evolve into The Man that you've been trying to stick it to.

3. Grief is an accumulation of snow. Shovel it out of your immediate path, but it still sits piled high in the front yard, providing a chilling reminder of its presence.

4. During social events, take on the heavy lifting if the conversation sags. When gaps in dialogue are unavoidable, meet the eyes of other people indifferently. Hold, then release.

5. Negativity is emotional pollution. You can't hang around places where it spews without inhaling its toxicity.

6. It's okay to be on the wrong train as long as you stay on the right track.

7. As people walk past you, they instinctively move as far away as possible. They think you're a threat. We all believe the other person is a threat.

8. Bigotry is society's eternal boomerang, destined to return no matter how often we toss it away.

9. Do not confuse thirst with the desire to fill oneself and not remain empty. Especially at bars.

10. If you cannot be honest, become a mystery.

11. Asking for directions from those who have never been where you're going is a surefire strategy to get lost.

12. Every party has a pooper. Make them pick up their shit and leave.

13. Become skilled in more than one thing. One-trick ponies rarely get encores.

14. People will hold the past against you like a blade to your neck. Resist the urge to flinch. Never get cut.

15. Don't drown in the undercurrent of the avoidable while swimming away from what's unavoidable.

16. Make sure anyone trying to prey on you starves.

BLUES NOTE NO. 2

Dear Blues,

Your beat shuffles beneath my skin, its percussion banging against my inner machinery. My mental light bulbs flicker for weeks, dust thick in all the sockets. Sugar in spaces no one dares kiss. After midnight, my thoughts grow slick with intention as secrets fall open atop beds like suitcases. Lewdly sticking my fingers in places they don't belong. The blues become a crowded concept. Overfilled, like that closet we cram everything into until its door cannot close. Downtown, I wear shoes that blister my heels, sorrow rising to the surface whenever misfortune rubs too hard or just hard enough. Indulgence becomes ritual, shitfaced on rum every Saturday night, my smile darkening with each dirty riddle. Doubt chafing my confidence. This beautiful mess of genetic tendencies and homegrown awkwardness. Listen to the voices reveal how the shadow of my family tree shades my infrastructure. Prodigal uncles and deadbeat cousins. The evil twin I may or may not have strangled inside the womb, his duality stalking me from the flipside of existence, hellbent on retribution.

Code Switchin' on Fo-Fos, or, It Takes Grindin' to Be a King

An obligatory silent nod of affirmation
cubicles ain't never been for black folk
capitalist cellblocks where none dare
defy gatekeepers screening for ethnicity
in exploratory interviews—hide your glare
become whoever you need to be
at this moment, though this moment has
equity drowning in a sea of stereotypes
sermons on repeat, endless loops of
gaining the world but losing soul
each time you reach God, you unbecome
what it do after banging your skull against
heaven resurrected in the flesh as
vultures who swallow themselves whole
despite the deferred promotions
a lot of haters and a lot of homies

to the other black guy at the firm, who knows
as one brother gets hired, so shall a nigga be fired
ask HR how many successfully creep around
in slush piles of cover letters and resumes, and
then smile just enough to get an offer
since you're just tryin' to get over
Superfly steeped in your royal blood
proper syntax staining your tongue, and
scripture about the meek inheriting everything
that doesn't quite fit this narrative, but know
not much fits nor breaks except glass
ceilings—take this lonely token of
a performance review of corporate culture
and wonder why you stay employed
adrift rudderless amongst coworkers
some friends and some phony

Speak so Well

People say you speak so well. Every phrase numbly enunciated to hide traces of pain. Diction scrubbed clean of the struggle with rags and spray bottles of the strongest disinfectant linguistic camouflaging can buy. All day your words hold value if spoken with your milk voice. All day they rub against frustration, daring friction to kindle flames. When you speak so well, you can become an exception to typecasting, sometimes. Like language is a suit you hang in your closet every evening and take out each morning. Eventually, flat dialogue floats towards deaf ears just because, because in the end, you don't belong, and there's no guaranteed way to be heard, to know for sure they listen, to feel respected as your syllables get whitewashed with a smile.

MY DELAYED RESPONSE TO YOUR OUTRAGE AT MY HOODIE THAT SAYS *BLACK LIVES MATTER*

Perhaps the concept of compassion
can only appear after acts of callousness.

Perhaps the idea of inclusion only
gets noted by those in the margins.

Perhaps thoughts of caring
arise only after refusing to give
a fuck about other people.

Perhaps you should listen as I whisper
grace into the ears of the wicked—
even if my words may sting.

I hope this message reaches you
in time. Perhaps empathy could come
first. Perhaps your peace cannot be
found until I unearth mine.

Perhaps mercy could shine light
on the shade in your soul.

Perhaps you hear an imaginary threat
concealed in the written declaration
that my existence has relevance,
and the resentment you display
comes from overlooking my value
before you acknowledge yours.

ELEGY AFTER ANOTHER HATE CRIME

The best way to preach the gospel of life
is to sing its praises in the presence of death.
If you do not agree, then don't. This much seems
certain: a bigot fires his rifle inside a supermarket,
executing innocents for the pigment of their skin.
Afterwards, silence, or whatever sorrow calls itself
once bullets pierce flesh, stumbled into the scene
like a clumsy supporting actor. Then the scene
became just another familiar scene. Fade to black.

It is midday. I am on a couch. My smartphone
buzzes with numbing news. A sadness settles in
about this shooting and I forget what defines me.
The darkness of a room on a clouded day, as it
swallows everything, says to remain still. This
afternoon, there will be nothing but mourning.

EXPLAIN TO ME THE BLUES AS IF I'VE NEVER HAD THEM

How things sit next to each other yet remain
completely separated. Forgettable street names
permanently embossed upon rusted sign panels,
a molasses-slow sunrise postponing daybreak,
bodies pressed against bodies while spawning
false intimacy on a commuter train, old photos
curled up out of vintage sadness. Summer exhaling,
waiting for autumn's cool arrival. The difference
between what we lose and what has been taken
from us, or the way the living darkness swallows
all the dying light. How someone might squander
a lifetime trying to mend what's unfixable instead
of building something new, or how the downhearted
never look up to enjoy the scenery on their journey,
or how a marriage erodes into a spouse being nothing
but a warm body on the cold side of a bed. How people
come to stay with one another, devoted yet disenchanted,
with no better reason than that's just how it's always been.
The melancholy of a creek during a drought, infuriated
by the decades it has flowed, only to run dry in the end.

BLUES NOTE NO. 3

Dear Blues,

When you were born, I became cerulean with light. My dreams seemed pristine and dazzling, with nary a cloud on the horizon. I kept you padlocked within the security box of my body, but you inevitably escaped. Translated temptation as if it were a second language and rolled dice in alleys, everything coming up snake eyes. You marveled at my sly tendency to pull feigned smiles from pockets like loose change. We made a confidence game of it, here then gone, then here again. Life felt heavier than it looked, like a rain-soaked blanket. On my knees in church, there were countless confessions. I filled infinity with them. As if infinity could evolve into a verb if we just infinitied it into existence. You crooned testimonials with careless lyrics as folks nodded off beat. I stayed behind to sort out the carnage. My integrity divided, again and again, splinters shot in all directions like fireworks.

An Introduction to Mansplaining

I might act like a gentleman, but my mouth
is an accomplice to countless criminal acts.

Every smile flashes a glimpse of baleful
intentions, teeth gleaming in the gaslight.

Under control and underhanded, I make
propositions while removing my belt, pull

compliments from my crotch, camber words
around common decency like bending spoons.

For a price, watch me silently fuck the futures
of those seeking appreciation and affection.

Seduction, snake charm, sweet deception.
I can speak nearly any desire into existence.

With excuses at my nimble fingertips, pluck
the folded notes of apology from my tongue.

FOR THE TATTOOED WOMAN AT LEFTY'S TAP

Because he broke your heart and left arm,
Vince is an inauspicious badge-
a five-letter caveat spanning the small of your back,
a de-facto advertisement of a troubled past
with a flair of cursive script. Between your backside
and the dragon scaling the arc of your spine,
his name rages, bridging across your vertebrae;
a ponytail swings down periodically to kiss his moniker,
touching the black-inked scar of suppressed remembrances,
tethering your deliberate evolution. He keeps you sleepless
with his afterimage, and each half-healed and martyred limb
aches for more of the fury he called love. His memory
touches your waistline like lustful hands. How simple
the pain that lines and decorates your body. How it fans,
blazes, writes itself anew with each tenuous sigh,
gossips about the issues you've turned your back on.

AN INCOMPLETE UNDERSTANDING OF LOVE, WITH ANNOTATIONS

Embarrassing confessions aside, love is a masochistic endeavor.[1] Consider that neighbor whose personal history is defined by a husband's absence and the memories of his fists.

All my life I've seen women sell themselves in one way or another just to survive. Sellers in name only; many pay the price then argue it's all worth the cost. Love is transitory enough for us to miss its presence yet motionless enough to mimic our stubbornness.[2] So collect compliments like trophies, swallow insults and shit them out as gold.[3] It's a valid coping mechanism, really.

A moment, together or apart, can define a relationship forever. Save the sweetest lies for yourself and tell everyone else the truth. Language without communication is a subtle form of sabotage. The problem lies not with silence, but with the words we force to fill it.[4]

Beware of kisses that approximate innocence. And the javelins we eventually sink into each other's hearts.[5] Do not apologize. Allow tension to linger in the house like the comfortable dust nobody's ever willing to clean.

Women can pick out the faults in a man like they're picking out chunks of unwanted tomato from a salad and then call it intuition because that sounds better than stereotyping. Whatever. I liken love to a helium balloon untethered, doubt to the open blue sky into which it quixotically floats. Keep rising and don't look down. Don't ever look down.

---

[1] You can't see it until it's already too late. The hunger for it gnawed at the corners of common sense. You're praising the grace of the unmade bed; restraint lost in the narrow space between the walls.

[2] We want to believe that without love, we'd all disappear. But in reality, without love, life goes on. We go on.

[3] Treat a person like a dog and eventually they'll bite.

[4] Sooner or later, a couple has nothing to say, swallow the needle and thread stitching them together.

[5] If the past is a rope hanging between us, it can tie a noose.

IF LOVE IS A BIG CITY, LATELY I'VE CONSIDERED RELOCATING

When she whispers lust into another man's ear at the bar, my mind
becomes a commuter train: screeching stops, graffiti-tagged doors

and, inside, a flickering fluorescence. Meanwhile, in the alleys
behind my sleep-deprived eyes, thoughts scatter like transients

at the sound of a police siren. I would have loved to take her
on a road trip where headwinds bully cars on rural highways

and we could imagine hope residing in the static between AM stations.
Now there's an entire nation full of motels where we'll never sleep—

together, at least. Not to mention nightclubs where we'll never dance
until closing time and diners where we'll never stumble in searching

for something salty to quell our booze-induced hunger. So be it. This city
is filled with constellations of starry-eyed fools orbiting people they claim

are their world, only to find themselves pulled into parallel universes
where they do things they'd never consider doing, normally. I recognize

the symptoms, pack up everything, and think about hightailing it
out of town. Ignore my cell phone's cranky ring, force her to leave

a catalog of regrets in the space between the voicemail's beep
and her tentative *goodbye*. Well goodbye, love. I'm moving on.

BLUES NOTE NO. 4

Dear Blues,

Often you come from nowhere, clutching hope like a toddler does their favorite toy. Mumbling harebrained ideas, conceived and repeated until they sound convincing. You loiter in the hallways of my mind, glowing, slightly blue. Sometimes, you hold onto a pint glass, joint, or pocketknife while skulking in the shadows. No matter what, you stay uncontrollable and inconsolable. Polluted by the emotional byproduct of all the women I did dirty just to get over one from the past. How I occasionally played fast and loose with the whole honesty thing, circles of double talk sullying my reputation, siphoning away trust equity. The students I swindled over summer breaks for tuition money, our long rides south of nowhere in the dead of night. Call a hustle what it is. Slick talk or parlor tricks suspending common sense in purgatory. Self-fulfilling prophecies tethered to lyrics that sound authentic but aren't. Yet I sing, nonetheless.

PANDEMIC POSTCARD

You wonder how to center yourself in an off-balanced world,
how to watch everything fall apart but pretend it's still intact.

I could ask the same: how can our world take social and distancing,
thrusting those words together clumsily like they're on a blind date,

making them glance off each other, two billiard balls that touch
briefly before heading off in different directions? Or watch idly

as gaslighting torches our collective sanity, charlatan leaders
on social media claiming there's nothing to see here, despite

our vision catching more fires than we care to witness: contagion,
fractured economies, the vain attempts to scrub away our nation's

long stain of injustice. In the year of the disease, we had nothing
more to lose until we completely lost it. One thing after another,

gone, feeling connected only to our devices and desperation,
all smiles emptied or hidden behind masks. As society's seams

unravel, we lose more than just our time and patience. Do you see
what just happened, how I started off tiptoeing through minefields

of uncertainty towards a flattened curve and wound up starting
uprisings within my soul, igniting the fuse of my incendiary heart?

Social distancing: perhaps it doesn't separate us after all.
Maybe it brings us closer, in theory, collectively fighting

the urge to give in to touch, forcing us to forsake our plans,
having learned long ago to want only what we cannot have.

A BEGINNER'S GUIDE TO SIN

I.   After assassinating your faith, savor the contact high
        from the gun's secondhand smoke. Exhale, then cough
        out any residual innocence. Recognize what bruises
        already know — your damaged heritage, its aching
        reminders of your conflicted interior. You now belong to
        the fire of careless desire.

II.   Lose your religion or identity — find a cocktail napkin
        and doodle frantically, knowing what idle hands
        eventually become. Stop preaching sermons to the
        emancipated horizon since reality ritually harasses the
        backside of every dream.

III.   Your lies become a homily, a desperate incantation of
        half-drowned hallelujahs resurfacing, gasping for air. Be
        the most honest hymn people will ever sing but realize
        they might still condemn your lyrics.

IV.   As a street preacher shrieks Armageddon soliloquies,
        you hope for an antidote to commonplace chaos yet revel
        in the tiny apocalypses of daily life, the bumper crop of
        success harvested from seeds of deceit, how longing and
        envy only make good on promises at a price.

V.   The desire to affix meaning to desire is a self-fulfilling
        prophecy. The feedback loop echoes a somber testament
        atop the mountain we go tell it on.

VI.   Stop clutching the talisman of other's beliefs when
        what's wrong feels liberating. An open mouth often talks
        its way into a closed casket. An open mouth becomes a
        wound that never closes, never heals, never whispers
        amen.

VII.   Forget scripture—with its shaky walls and rickety
        bridges, its cracked foundation jerry-rigged with prayers.
        Praise the spilled liquor staining the nights with 100-
        proof roadmaps to false redemption, until mattresses
        reluctantly weep their solemn confessions. Until
        unfaithful spouses bow their heads, begging for
        forgiveness.

Theorems of Desire

If Friday night, then $a = implication$. b will equal the backseats of cars, proportional to infinitesimal moments between gropes.

In a bathroom, water temperature is a function of entropy and seduction. Therefore, $b = body\ heat$, but only if a two-person shower is assumed to be a closed system.

If aroused, then $action \neq logic$. If consenting, then a will roughly equal the distance separating fingertip from breast but divided by the surface area of any remaining clothing.

Assume sloe gin and compliments, infer flirtatious gestures. Then subtract the body's weight in lust, or better, deduct the age when your virginity was misplaced.

In bed, b^2 always equals tongue.

On Mondays, a can equal the workplace, which also implies noontime tryst.

If unexpected, then $a = phone\ call$. $a + b$ occasionally equals *love*, but only after midnight. If so, b will nearly always equal *affection, or regret*.

BLUES NOTE NO. 5

Dear Blues,

It is so very American of you to blame others for your blunders. To blame solutions for the existence of problems, or victims for crimes. You fill troubled minds with hollow notes, twelve bars at a time. Fill night's void with echoes of moonlight and moonshine. Nothing inside, and then everything. So very precise of me to make a refrain of it. So cliché. I plagiarized that from you, my obscene obsession with call-and-response schemes and chord progressions. Explaining how tough times always seem to track folks down, even after they've changed for the better. How lies rest clumsily on the tongue long after being spoken. How love gets abused like an untrained house pet, scolded at the slightest hint of disobedience. How grief slowly settles over optimism like dust on windowsills. How uncertainty grows so large that it swallows us all if we let it.

A Collection of What-Ifs

What if the best feeling isn't getting a lap dance
with a dirty martini in hand but instead waking up

to a blackout sky so dark not even the moon dares
to shine? What if a person and their shame stay

inseparable, and our bodies are just warehouses
to stockpile guilt for safekeeping? What if the dirt

under our fingernails proves to the world that the work
we do must be real? What if there are no additional

insults to dole out or punches to throw which also
means everybody's nametag should read *Hello*

My Name is ~~Human~~? What if lust is a trapdoor
we try to shut tight, but its frame keeps swelling

as everything does in this blasted summer humidity?
What if sore throats are our bodies' way of coaching

us to continue screaming the truth, even if it stings?
What if we cannot care about hope because it keeps

ditching us when it's needed most? What if we all
took a needle and thread and stitched our mouths

into synthetic smiles until society sliced through
the seams? What if we collected enough lies so

we could build a bridge to the outskirts of honesty,
which is one way to ask *What if we don't want any*

of this, What if our souls were born to float away,
and *What if we go on and on and on without finding*

answers? What if we are merely the sum of all our
mistakes, and those screwups beget a sadness

we can never escape, never whittle into submission?
What if booby traps lurk beneath every sin, and we are

all destined to become ensnared, which also means
we could potentially escape? What if we never do?

A LIST OF STATEMENTS THAT
REQUIRE VALIDATION

1. Silence is the official language of survival.

2. The ring slides back on the finger as easily as it slides off.

3. Living, by definition, is a death-defying act.

4. Maybe means maybe not.

5. The security is adequate.

6. Lovemaking requires the presence of love.

7. This hurts me more than it hurts you.

8. Stop trying and everything becomes effortless.

9. Listen closely and you can hear the cracks inside of explanations.

10. Some things you just can't get back.

11. Hell is a crowded, endless bus commute in July.

12. I will always be there, I love you, et. al.

13. The tap water is safe to drink.

14. Her panties are (a) cotton, (b) crotchless, or (c) missing.

15. Pain can be the loveliest aphrodisiac.

16. No question is a dumb question.

17. The police will protect us.

18. Duct tape can fix anything.

19. Debt goes away if you ignore it.

20. The perception of authority begets arrogance.

21. Guilt is a straitjacket that hinders you from moving forward.

22. I can quit whenever I want to.

EXCERPT FROM AN INTERVENTION LETTER

Most evenings you dwell in that narrow space between ardor and anger, reciting Shakespeare and smashing all the dishes. At intervals, drinking every beer in the apartment and stumbling down the stairs. It's scary how much you wander for your age, blacking out and waking up in some other zip code. Each night out becomes an excuse to cuss out some loathsome doll who had it coming. Some bartender diluting drinks. Some Ken doing Barbie wrong. The bystanders triggered, intoxicated witnesses to the sobering aftermath as you become a typhoon of expletives and cleavage. By morning, you trash every memory, even of our make-up sex. The creamer sours and I burn the bacon to black. You top your morning coffee off with vodka while I lean toward the imaginary knife you hold to my throat.

BLUES NOTE NO. 6

Dear Blues,

Occasionally hints of a better life flicker at the edges like a dying campfire. A fresh start, a new home, a dream job. The perfect match with their obvious red flags. Sometimes hope aches like a phantom limb or a childhood injury that refuses to mend right. You keep an assortment of unfulfilled promises on a bedside table, and after midnight, they buzz with fervor. The average person has four to six dreams nightly, so some are bound to be ludicrous. How do we know unless we've fact-checked them for feasibility? How to know with certainty their validity? It rains, it pours, and the best-laid plans get screwed. Things fall apart, schemes come together, and the sun rises and sets. And then there's you, with half-healed wings spreading in the stratosphere, gliding recklessly, Icarus-high on desire. Slinging yourself into gravity's untrustworthy grasp, singing life's praises while sidestepping its scourges. Feigning invincibility while knowing everything crashes, eventually.

EDUCATION

Properly touching a female, she said, is akin
to the complex task of refolding an open map

or unraveling the knot of complicated feelings
that accompanies love in the age of HIV (long pause

that sounded like fear). It's not a sin to pray aloud
for more than a mundane wash-rinse-and-repeat life

with the saliva-moistened halos of our mouths
and it's not a crime to crave hearing the echo

of our rum-sweetened names moaned repeatedly
within the dark architecture of back seats:

her neck arched beautifully backwards,
throat vulnerable to my judgmental kiss.

Voiceless, I became Technicolor blue, past tense.
Weighted by vertigo and hundred-proof logic.

The realization that when your woman opens up
like a wound, you are obligated to be the stitch.

UNSOLICITED ADVICE RECEIVED DURING MY WEDDING RECEPTION

Sometimes it's smart to stay silent rather than win an argument.
You'll sleep better in your bed than on the couch. Be dependable,

but not boring. She has control, of course, but you do have influence
if you decide to wield it. Which is to say, act like a man and your wife

will respect your manhood. Just be confident and she'll follow your lead,
during waltzes and in life. Who knows why? Women are like TV channels.

Eventually, you have to pick just one, so choose one you enjoy watching.
Ignore all the other fish in the sea swimming past you. Please enunciate

when speaking into the microphone. Keep your own bank account. Hold
down a decent job. Buy her flowers, but only when it's not predictable.

Pray together and you'll stay together. Bad news sounds a bit sweeter
when it's punctuated by a kiss. Two Geminis means four personalities

under one roof, so beware. You're both go-getters, but someone still
needs to be the homemaker. Don't drink too much. Try not to put on

too much weight. Don't have kids too soon. If she goes on the pill,
her boobs will get bigger. Don't do anything that results in regret.

She could do better. You could do worse. Grandma would've loved
the ceremony if she was alive. Stand up straight or you'll look short

in the pictures. If you don't smile, people will think you're unhappy.
A happy wife makes for a happy life. Always keep the gift receipt.

CONFESSIONAL

Before long, I agree to be the villain in this play, but only if I can stay out too late and skirt my responsibilities. You give me countless second chances and final ultimatums before I go off-script. Off-balance. Off the subject. Off-key. Mistake apologies for opportunities to make questionable behavior a routine occurrence. Everything I know about our home is hard. Hard choices. Hard water that makes my skin impossibly dry and leaves the showerhead chalky. Hard liquor makes hard luck more palatable sometimes. Our vows are a revolver pressed against my temple, keeping my demons at bay. All wandering eyes until the open mouth of my desire grows so wide that it swallows everything in sight. Somehow, I agree to come back and be the hero instead, but this time I renege on promises in the second act and keep stepping on your cues. My intentions stay tangled like extension cords in the basement, forgotten and collecting dust.

TO PROCRASTINATE UNPACKING BOXES IN MY APARTMENT, I SEE A TARANTINO FLICK

on its second run in a discount theater
with the enthusiasm of a fan on opening

night. In case you haven't seen the film,
I will not spoil the plot twist, though what

is there really to spoil since every storyline
is a blatant rehash of some other narrative,

but let's just say a hero turned heel exactly
when you would imagine a betrayal to occur.

Depending on how you define dishonesty,
the ending was unsurprising. My divorce

was not finalized when a stack of papers
were signed, notarized, and processed.

It happened days later, when I ran into her
friend at a cinema lobby concession stand,

and, with popcorn in hand and sincere eyes,
she proclaimed *you're probably better off.*

ONE LAST POEM ABOUT DIVORCE

It is apparent now there are no endings,
just beginnings that like winters flourish,
then vanish, and then, when the time comes,
reappear as autumn's faint warmth wanes.
Hope doesn't even end when one gets hit
by hard times: a layoff, an eviction, a trial
separation. It just dilutes, transforms, and,
at most, grows distant. I thought a world after you
would be a world without you, but here you are
humming within every memory, whistling
in the background of each whispered prayer,
you who have always found some way
to meddle with everything, even joy.

BLUES NOTE NO. 7

Dear Blues,

If we lie perfectly still in the dark, we can pretend we are twins. Our clothes reeking of tequila and secrets. The stress coiled in our stomachs is the same stress, with the same nagging burn. Morning gives us the silent treatment from the bed where we sleep, side by side, holding our breath. In our mouths, the same cavities, the same collection of fillings twinging with a lust for dulcet things. The same madness rattling in our throats. Truth is, I never liked mimicking others all that much, but you and me, we're just like *this*. Which is to say, spitting images or dead ringers. I think it, and you confess it. You wonder, so I inquire, interrogate, insist. I believe it, so you keep chucking rocks at it, hoping it breaks. If we lie perfectly still, no one can tell us apart except for the sheet music you stash between the mattress and box spring. How folks call you spiritual and label me as a free spirit. They frighten me with their resentment. Their sideways glances and gossip. Morning screeches like an unwatched teakettle. Like a twin, I may not want to be like you, but I am. The more I understand this, the more I am at peace.

EIGHT THINGS YOU MIGHT NOT KNOW ABOUT MY CLONE

1.
My clone was that adolescent friend
who would come over after school
every day but became uber-popular
in high school and then experimented
with drugs and later went off the grid
but now is back in town trying to get
their shit together and we have coffee
and catch up one afternoon before
night classes at the community college.

2.
I have grown resentful of my clone
for writing the groundbreaking novel
that I lack the audacity and discipline
to author myself, but then not caring
enough to attempt to get it published.

3.
My clone was in an indie band.
Mildly successful with a cult following
in the brief post-Napster, pre-iPod era.
Even toured several Midwestern cities
and paid off student loans with the proceeds.
Later, in downtown Des Moines, my clone
quit abruptly over creative differences
while claiming they penned all the band's
cliched songs. It may have been the truth,
but it was bad form. Afterward, neither
my clone nor the talentless remainder
of the group found anything near their
original success. Post bygones, they do
get together, occasionally, for random
one-offs at dive bars – but only after
a debt collector or ex-wife has called
one of them demanding payments.

4.
My clone's inner circle is an exclusive
nightclub. It's not that no one can get inside—
it's just that you need to be on the list.

5.

My clone did a ton of self-work to foster
personal growth while embarking on
many journeys, literal and metaphorical,
to arrive here. My clone squandered their
stamina while going the distance and has
been heaving for breath ever since
but remains focused on the finish line.
After their glow-up, they endured
constant eye rolls and sneers from haters.
It's hard work being so well-adjusted,
but if my clone did it, then you can, too.

6.

My clone represents an advanced form
of sentient technology from a dystopian
future, and they will singe your thoughts
if you try to read their mind. Be careful.

7.

My clone doesn't care much about
what you want. My clone doesn't care
much about what I want, either.

8.

My clone has a love child that I kindly
clothe, feed, and watch over whenever
my clone feels a bit too downhearted
or distracted to care. My clone's bastard
is hard-headed like me, so I give them
heavy-handed life advice while playing
catch in the backyard, hugging them
after they misjudge the trajectory
of my cut fastball, touching their bruises
gently and chanting *it's going to be
okay* as they cry through their pain.

UNWANTED INHERITANCE

One summer, my father swallows depression. It camps in his throat as an emotional refugee. Family members take turns trying to pluck it out with elongated objects – tweezers, tongs, needle-nosed pliers. We touch it, sometimes, but never remove it, so it persists. Eventually, everyone pretends it doesn't exist, except for me. I hear depression lingering whenever my father screams about trivial things. Nobody else notices how it slinks around the periphery and rattles inside his esophagus. All day, it sings the blues. Through birthday parties, vacations, and graduations. All night, his depression sleeps with barely a peep and survives on menthol loosies and self-loathing. No one can convince me that it isn't real. That it isn't there. That it isn't scheming to crawl out one night, out of his mouth and into mine.

REDEMPTION ARC

My dad served in the Army for more than twenty years.
He wrote the lyrics to his blues throughout two wars, long
enough for him to stop lip-syncing someone else's songs.

And when he went to bars, he could say *Crown and Coke*
until the words rotted inside his mouth like a sweet tooth
and they'd still pour him another. During those two decades

and change, he had one wife, briefly. After that, he had another,
and later my mother, and then came me, his unexpected son.
We all asked him to be better than he was. But things never work

that way. You can't expect a live grenade to never explode.
And if he's back stateside from Vietnam and eleven years later
still hollers out *Charlie's coming let's fucking move* in his sleep,

then he can identify the ghost of an enemy lurking in flashbacks
but cannot recognize one staring back at him from the mirror,
or detect the slow leak deflating his punctured confidence.

My father's favorite war story was silence—so many narratives
started then abruptly ended. A pregnant pause followed by
fierce eye contact with his only child and a gruff *ain't no place*

for a black man in a white man's army. As if that statement
exonerated him from the shouting, insults, and intimidation,
the friendly fire in our household. Often I wished he would talk

about the war, open the reservoir, allow the pain to flow out.
I would have cleaned up the mess afterwards, like all the broken
plates and jostled furniture of his tirades. But things never work

that way. You can't expect a live grenade to never explode.
We both liked to ask for what we knew we would never get—
closure—elusive as an apology from a bitter soldier.

My Therapist Says Smiling More Will Help Me

unwrap the blanket of indifference that has swaddled me
since birth. But explain that to the gravity pulling my spirits

downward and grounding my aspirations like planes in need
of repair, or mention that to the doubt loitering in my mind

like a ghost in a basement, restless and haunted by this new,
hollow habit of falsely flashing teeth. No one got the memo

that shedding my resting scowl would hypothetically shine
a low-watt light onto the dim confines of my inner thoughts

as God sews dusk into darkness, which, too, remains stitched
to the aesthetic of my nocturnal soul as it stirs like a compass

needle seeking the right direction. People claim I can cure
this contagion, that depression will surrender its weapons

and retreat limber-tailed back to the hell that spawned it,
but I know of no devil who would willingly banish itself

without invoking turmoil as part of its exit strategy. And still,
on the days I do savor life, the sunrise leaves me stunned

like a random hello from a cranky neighbor who usually cares
less. On the days I do savor life, I hope the fog of the past

lifts and gives way to clearer vision, so I can finally see
how flowers bloom even in times of despair. Every day

above ground should be cherished, so my mouth becomes
a closed casket for the complaints that die inside it, unsaid,

despite their yearning to be resurrected and uttered. I get
so enlightened that I glow in the dark. I ache for happiness

to etch itself in black and white, but remain disappointed
as it arrives uncertain and grey, synthetic as my forced smile.

BLUES NOTE NO. 8

Dear Blues,

At birth, you get named *spirituals*. Then *work songs*, then *field hollas,* with a working-class *a* on its backside instead of a prim and proper *er*. Your cradle slowly fills with names, cast off like old clothes. You amplify into *shouts* and *chants*, but neither quite fit. *Ballads* and *folk songs* seem too shallow for your depth. Tired of those trite descriptions lulling you to sleep, people try labeling you with words that reflect the verity of your aesthetic—*sadness, melancholy, despondence. Depression* sounds melodramatic, yet it somehow suits you. That is until the rumormongers start casting their disapproving looks toward you. Folks say the more vivid the name, the better the prospects. So, the world props you back up and christens you the *blues*, and we all know how that turns out. A custom-made moniker with a trinity of meaning that braids color with musicality and mood—a perfect match.

MEDITATION DURING A MASK MANDATE

I wake up and morning suffocates my soul.
I draw the blinds as dawn's silence grows

deafening. I tentatively ride the commuter train,
walk past buildings, and remain a CDC-sanctioned

distance from the guys wearing power ties
and frowns like corporate merit badges.

The flight of pigeons, the sad encampment of tents
in the park, sidewalk vendors hawking counterfeit

purses, and endless litter all hijack my hopes. A lucky
man on a street corner gets to sing his blues. This city

is ghosting me, gradually, drowning itself in a sea
of gentrification. There's this dream I have in which

I love the world, and it chooses to love me back,
sometimes, like a disgruntled spouse. I explore it

from start to finish, like how my fingers touch a new
library book. There are no limits, only wind. Like you,

I was created out of desperation. Like you, I was baptized
into the religion of optimism, blindly pledging allegiance

to the vague existence of better days ahead. Head in the
clouds, hand over my heart. Hand over my foolish heart.

RX FOR THE BLUES

Ingredients: Fractured epiphanies of infinite longing. The wrong side of every flipped coin. The seductive pull of self-destruction. Imagine your darkest desire stewing in a potful of its juices. Some might swallow it reluctantly like medicine. Others would pour it down the drain like curdled milk.

Benefits: The ability to shake song from silence. Awestruck, you'll fall onto a soft mattress of sorrow. Everything will feel bruised and tender, but pain can be an effective teacher. Recommended for when you're walking alone through bad neighborhoods or hell without an exit strategy or backup plan.

Before Using This Drug: Know your family history and whether you come from a long line of malcontents. Some may covet the shine of your enthusiasm; others will shear emotions from their roots via casual sarcasm. Conversations or confrontations may occur.

Usage: Follow instructions carefully. Imagine a bass line, a guitar riff. Lyrics will come as needed. You'll find them at the bottom of every shot glass. Store the words on your person, concealed so no one can pickpocket them.

Caution: You will no longer speak softly at church. All roads will lose their signs. You'll be prone to strange weather and temptation in tight dresses. Stand firm, or you'll be knocked over.

Overdose: If the suggested dosage is exceeded, immediately induce vomiting with hard liquor. Learn to fight, fuck, or flee without hesitation. Dance or cry like nobody's watching. If ingested in error, happiness may deteriorate, the way some marriages get whittled down over time like driftwood.

Side Effects: You may become a badass who can sing dead money back to life. Resurrect faith from its unmarked grave. Pry hope out from a pawnbroker's crooked grip. Make sense without logic. Graffiti your signature anywhere using pen, paint, or pocketknife.

ALL WE ASK FOR

I've got the end of the world scribbled on my face
and cheap beer clinging to my breath.
Carpe Noctem, motherfucker.
An incarnate cliché of lonesomeness, drinking by myself
and wondering how long it's been since I last ate
a home-cooked meal. All we ask for is what we cannot have:
chances to redeem sorrows, band-aids for our gashed egos,
a way to keep all our fears inside, packed cellophane tight.
The ponytailed bartender keeps glancing at her watch
as if she expects a miracle to arrive at the top of the hour,
some timely phenomenon that might rescue her
from a lifetime of pouring beer and relying on tip money
to pay bills. I'm tempted to offer words to lift her spirits,
encouragement for her to push forward and never shrink
back. But my face is not a kind one, and I've seen her snarl
at the customers she perceives are making passes at her.
So instead, I read a stranger's scribbles in the back of a bar
and become as anonymous as that graffiti. How pathetic
to be a name on this wall, to have your identity
etched on this table. Another mug arrives and already
I have envisioned the alcohol flowing down my throat,
tinkering with my good sense. This time tomorrow
you might find me sober. Cursing the future
I predicted but continued with anyway–hope hanging
like a leather jacket on a hook by the door.

AND WHAT GOOD ARE ALL THOSE THOUGHTS AND PRAYERS

if our world keeps falling apart? After all, no one can even recall
why the flags remain at half-staff, which means we are either

suffocating our memories or letting our memories smother us.
We live only by that which still allows us to survive. The flag,

for instance, triggers us to either sense pride or grief, depending
on how high it flies and what news keeps trending on the internet.

I suppose we are being carefully asphyxiated by our recollections:
online troll postings, bodycam footage, school shootings devised

by tormented souls who execute others to ease their pain and when
their aches persist, they turn a gun on themselves and their suicides

become symbolic of our country. We might pledge allegiance to
whatever windblown fabric we must in order to continue breathing

with knees pressed against our necks. We may stand and salute as
the anthem gets played, knowing we remain victims of a recycled

melody. We listen as the flag flails in the breeze and we whistle back
in memory of a buried friend who didn't make the headlines.

Here we are, again, our mouths agape in shock and awe. Synthetic
outrage gets passed off as genuine emotion. Maybe things have

always been this way, and we've just recently grown disenchanted
with feigning optimism. We witness far too many tragedies to know

when the mourning should cease. People claim the first wholly
American style of music to gain traction and recognition across

the world was the blues. Maybe it's because the blues speak
of sunshine and storms from the same mouth. Maybe it's because

each refrain feels like another late-night prayer kneeling on the line
between life sentence and death penalty. Maybe it's because they

preach two-headed sermons, spitting scripture and blasphemy
in the same breath. If we keep singing the same blues, this nation

will become nothing but water and sky. Polluted, in memory of
whoever, our blood will run forever, these blues will never die.

EXPLAIN TO ME THE BLUES AS IF I'VE NEVER HAD THEM [REDACTED]

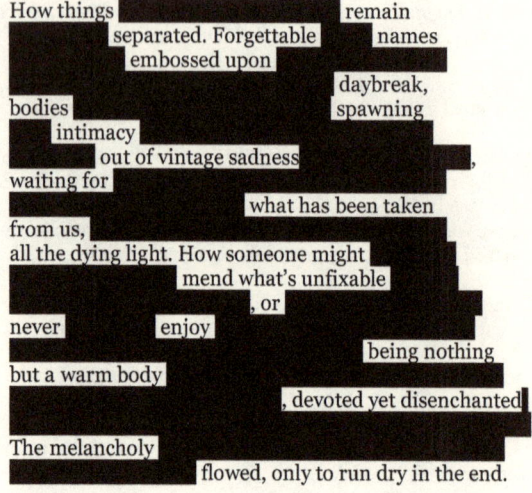

How things ▮▮▮▮▮ remain ▮▮▮▮▮ separated. Forgettable ▮ names ▮▮ embossed upon ▮▮▮▮ ▮▮ daybreak, bodies ▮▮▮▮ spawning ▮ intimacy ▮▮ out of vintage sadness ▮, waiting for ▮▮▮ what has been taken from us, ▮▮ all the dying light. How someone might ▮ mend what's unfixable ▮, or never ▮ enjoy ▮▮▮ being nothing ▮ but a warm body ▮▮ ▮, devoted yet disenchanted ▮. ▮ The melancholy ▮▮ flowed, only to run dry in the end.

BLUES NOTE NO. 9

Dear Blues,

You erase me in increments. Edit portions of my identity like needless dialogue in a draft novel. Fingers first, then toes. After deleting my aching knees, you cross out my reckless mouth, and then my scattered mind. Next, thinning hair and missing teeth. Admittedly, I've always been a five-o-clock shadow in rooms filled with respectable, clean-shaven gentlemen. Trouble in taverns always spots me, sidles up sweetly on barstools to whisper motel room numbers in my ear. Nowadays, my eyes stay cloudy as rivers outside, muddied and polluted. Your eyes roll endlessly at my antics. Claim I mention music too often in my writing. But I savor the sound of your name spelled out-B-L-U-E-S-and how each letter slides out my lips. Falls from my mouth and floats away. You grow bored with my hesitancy; how low spirits meld with high hopes. I scribble down several pensive metaphors. They're lovely but too convoluted. I learn to skip whatever semantics I use to pimp meaning out of nothing. No matter what song I dream of singing, you're what I'm stuck with.

Lamentation

Most days, life remains a believable hoax. Temptation casts its shadow around you like a tree. Your throat grows sore with prayers and pleas. Have mercy. Like leaves in the bellies of silkworms, something raw within your dark interior can produce something that shimmers for the world to covet. Do not be fooled by the mirage of blue-skied sunrises destined to dissolve into overcast afternoons. Or become enthralled with the knife tucked beneath your mattress for protection. While drifting through fever dreams, imagine your fingers grasping at the branches full of crabapples as they tap against the bedroom window. Front porches littered with beer bottles and cigarette filters. How each day your soul pours out like water until you return home, emptied.

GENTRIFICATION

Looking in the mirror,
I notice things have changed
with my beard.

A burgeoning populace
of white hairs have now
secured prime, highly visible
real estate in what used to be
an all-black neighborhood
for as long as anyone
can remember.

They've taken up residence
with no regard to history
or tradition, displacing darker
strands that were there
first, methodically annexing
properties, one follicle at a time,
changing the complexion
of the community,
and there's not a damn thing
I can do to stop it.

TERMS AND CONDITIONS FOR MODERN EXISTENCE

I won't claim to possess this body, though
I do shave its persistent stubble, adorn it
with designer clothes, and dutifully clean
and feed it. Mostly it seems contented,

though many nights it remains awake,
insomniac thoughts buzzing with anxiety
This body paces halls and sits awkwardly
at work. Is our agreement rent-to-own?

Or is my soul a squatter, an unauthorized
tenant making an exquisite mess of my life,
smashing valuables and stealing moments
until its inevitable eviction? When I vacate,

will another wayfaring traveler choose
to unlawfully inhabit this mortal vessel,
make it a home for their restless spirit?
Will I regret leaving? And will my final

breath be for the fear that wouldn't let me
ignore common sense and warning letters,
frenzy my voice into a triumphant howl, and
keep trespassing 'til the cops come knocking?

EPILOGUE

After you age into a scratched record. After you quash the eternal insurrection in your throat. After patience wears away like a blister on your hands. After your vigor fades like old pamphlets on bulletin boards. After dreams get abandoned like dead birds in the gutters of tract homes. After you drown in the river of other people's expectations, silently. After your light has shined long after it wanes like a dying star. After you learn how to forgive, but don't. After the ghosts of your confidence drift at night, beheaded and aimless. After you evolve into the finale of your narrative, an unexpected conclusion, an abrupt *fin* while the screen grows dark as life's ending.

BLUES NOTE NO. 10

Dear Blues,

By the end of your set, you've told the crowd all the best stories. Like the one with the lady fed up with her spouse's shenanigans, greeting him on the porch with sass and a shotgun. Or the one about a guy who falls so low that he does anything to get high. A running chronicle of dustups, screwups, and breakups. You seem downbeat and repetitive, but like a compelling narrator, you toss your entire soul into each tale, ducking loan sharks and sneaking out windows. Your charm gets drinks on the house and occasional for-a-good-time phone numbers. You're particular about distinguishing between a hard-scrabble existence, commonplace struggles, and your favorite—shit luck—which always leaves chaos in its wake. But worse, the vibe, which remains liable for your full heart and troubled spirit. For flat tires and absentee lovers. You're being overdramatic again, but you know no other way. When you leave, you're never really gone, just lingering in the background harvesting source material for the next album. The next curtain call. The next goodbye.

SELF-EULOGY, OR A NOTE FROM MY DEAD SELF

My story starts not where the bullet pierces flesh
but where the blood pools all around. Some waves
of pain never stop, no matter how well one writes
of healing. My story starts symbolically as a mirror
in front of which I knot my necktie, half-Windsor,
the way my late father taught me years ago, before
some other funeral. And so, my story starts with
a familiar version of grief constricting my throat.
In the church, I mutter something to myself that's
partway between prayer and curse. I have no truth
to offer as hazardous as this—everyone wants
their lives fixed, but nobody wants to do the work
to repair them. I was most like the bullet when I
viewed life as a series of transient moments, but I've
settled down now. No one buries kinfolk or comrades
with a smile, especially after happiness becomes
a fugitive that evades us. Here's another folded flag
atop the mantle. A new hashtag for social media.
A care package at the doorstep. Often a person only
gets called a victim once, and then they vanish.
The bluest note punctuates life's ballad. Find hope,
not just for hope's sake, but for how it disappears
without warning like a deadbeat relative. This is
how I plan to leave this life. Unceremoniously
as I came into it at birth, screaming out my tears
at a world overrun with ungrateful souls. My story
starts with a handful of well-meaning intentions
that I have since callously chucked out car windows
like roadside litter. I confess—I was not that good
of a person, but maybe I was good enough for you.

Invocation for the Mourning

Sometimes grief rises again unexpectedly
like the undead, reanimated, its corpse

zombie-stomping through your thoughts
haphazardly, humming extinction songs

and threatening to gnaw on your brain,
but do not move forward heavyhearted

or hide, instead continue with sure steps,
proceed with solace, knowing wherever

their spirit migrated is a better place for
them, now, believe they went knowingly,

aware of their previous place in this world
and in your heart, and arrived realizing that

they deserve serenity, departed the chaos
of human existence wide-eyed and roused

like a domesticated animal released into
the wild, a feral soul, primal and carefree,

realize they loosened their earthly shackles
with a free mind and newfound peace, so

no, do not carry the heavy cargo of sorrow
for the remainder of your life, brooding

and emotionally imploding, just promise
to keep on keeping on until you just can't.

EVERYBODY SINGS THE BLUES, SOMETIMES

Spinning, we shut our restless eyes
and recite prayers until evil is no longer
subletting space inside our thoughts.

Permafrost hearts thaw, melt like ice
cubes doused with hooch, while ambition
drowns in our lukewarm excuses. Hope is

a bullet lodged in our chests. It makes us
bleed out until sanity fades and dreams
collect dust like the B-sides in a jukebox.

We repeat mistakes ad nauseam until
we collapse. Bodies grow numb to our
bruised histories: our eyes tell stories

no one cares to read. How sadness
burrows in our bones, dissolves
into the marrow. Remember youth,

the bliss of foolishness, the ghosts
of promises once spoken haunting
our ears. Struggle fills a man's heart

yet leaves his soul empty as the
compliments he craves. We're suckers,
trusting the propaganda factory

in our minds. The burden of a tentative
future is discovering how wrong we were
about the past. Here we are, piss drunk

off our collective asses, life mixing
its usual cocktail of sadness and dazzle,
the first one's on the house. Maturity

is the hangover we're left to nurse
after another irresponsible night,
so many shots poured, motivation

sinking slowly to the bottom of each
glass. Listen to my frenzied music.
The overcast skies in my lyrics assume

you are familiar with pain but that you,
like me, are simply trying to endure.
Everybody sings the blues, sometimes.

Human detritus, wasting years tearing
ourselves apart to fit into narratives
we didn't even author. Reckless text

messages from some slurred hour
too late or too early to call.
Our mouths are answered prayers

for someone else's pleas, our fingers
so eager to please that their touch
feels like melted sin, heaven-sent.

Isn't it ironic how we confuse pretending
for persevering, grow comfortable as we
become contradictions? Ill-shaped hearts

beat within our chests, bloody & engorged,
versed in a darkness so deep only the moon
understands. Sadly, we know each other

only in pieces, but enough to recognize
some are missing, and the rest are taped
together, and even that tape is failing,

losing its grip, allowing pieces to fall
methodically, one by one. Our lives,
littered as they might be, are ready

to be picked up, floating in the narrow
space between positivity and despair.
Stumble awkwardly towards deliverance.

Our salvation finds itself half-spilled like
the drinks we toast to the blank pages
of our unfinished biographies. Cheers.

ERRATA FOR MY UNFINISHED BIOGRAPHY

p. 6, in the fourth sentence, before the word *childhood*, replace the word *quiet* with *awkward* or *disarranged*.

p. 36 and **p. 73**, in the paragraphs bookending the adolescent years, replace all subjunctive verbs with words that reflect remorse for what I should have tried, or better, embarrassment for not trying at all.

p. 107, When my father passed, the smirking professor's remark that I *made up his death to weasel out of finals* was unfounded, and thus the second paragraph should read:

After the test, the tequila and whiskey, sting and sour, poured smooth and somewhat pleasurably into my mouth. A grieving mind embraces vices while searching for relief, ready to plunge into error, to prevent getting pulled apart like a wishbone. Knuckles pop to the pressure of post-exam jitters as a paternal ghost haunts the corners of a barroom.

p. 125, third paragraph, sixth line, *tend to see the good in people* should read *am prone to loving trainwrecks, or becoming one myself.*

[This erratum more accurately reflects a debt to the co-authors of *My Divorce* and *Toxic Relationship #8* than to the books currently cited in Appendix C (missing).]

p. 166, first paragraph, second line, after the semi-colon, replace the phrase *in the morning* with *after four hours of threadbare sleep.*

p. 204, left column, replace all bulleted items with an inventory of moments when I observed or experienced discrimination yet stayed situationally silent, or a catalog of times when dangerous things accidentally got paired together, such as dulled hopes with sharp objects.

p. 268, after the fifth sentence, add the following statement:

The stranger with whom I'm workshopping poems says I'd be capable of great things if only I didn't hold back.

Appendix E, at the end of the section entitled *Repeated Mistakes*, replace *halfhearted apologies* with *sincere regrets*. Wherever logical, add the prefix un- to each adjective or verb listed.

Acknowledgments

Thank you to the editors who had faith in these poems and pieces, sometimes in different versions or with different titles, in the following places:

All My Relations, Volume 6 – "Dancing Machines"

2023 One Page Poetry Anthology – "My Therapist Says Smiling More Will Help Me"

Bacopa Literary Review – "Errata for My Unfinished Biography"

Bellingham Review – "Self-Eulogy, or a Note from My Dead Self"

The Broken Plate – "Theorems of Desire"

Collateral – "Redemption Arc"

Cutleaf Journal – "A Beginner's Guide to Sin," "Excerpt from an Intervention Letter," "To Procrastinate Unpacking Boxes in My Apartment, I Go See a Tarantino Flick," "One Last Poem about Divorce"

The Comstock Review – "Terms and Conditions for Modern Existence"

Dog Throat Review – "Blues Note No. 1," "Blues Note No. 3," "Blues Note No. 4," "Blues Note No. 6," "Blues Note No. 9," "Blues Note No. 10,"

Great Weather for Media – "My Delayed Response to Your Outrage at My Hoodie That Says *Black Lives Matter*"

Ginger Piglet – "A List of Statements that Require Validation"

Jet Fuel Review – "An Incomplete Understanding of Love, with Annotations"

The Lindenwood Review – "Speak so Well"

Medium – "Notes to Self on Self-Preservation"

Meetinghouse – "Blues Note No. 2," "Blues Note No. 5;" "Blues Note No. 7," "Blues Note No. 8"

MO: Writings on the River – "Defining the Blues"

Oakwood – "Mediation During a Mask Mandate," "Unwanted Inheritance"

Obsidian – "For the Tattooed Woman at Lefty's Tap"

Of Burgers & Barrooms, a Main Street Rag Anthology – "All We Ask For"

Oyster River Pages – "Everybody Sings the Blues, Sometimes," "Pandemic Postcard," "Ars Poetica, or Why I Drop Bombs aka Write Poems"

Penn Journal of Arts and Sciences – "If Life Is as Good as People Claim, Why Does It Feel Like I'm Just Waiting for Its Conclusion"

Red Coyote – "An Introduction to Mansplaining"

Rhino – "Code Switchin' on Fo-Fos, or It Takes Grindin' to Be a King"

Rigorous – "Explain to Me the Blues as if I've Never Had Them," "Elegy after Another Hate Crime," "Gentrification"

Route 7 Review – "Eight Things You Might Not Know about My Clone"

Switched-on Gutenberg – "A Partial Inventory of Personal Excuses"

Talking Stick – "Lamentation," "Unsolicited Advice Received During My Wedding Reception," "Epilogue"

Tidal Basin Review - "Education"

The Climax – "And What Good Are All Those Thoughts and Prayers"

The Tishman Review – "Rx for the Blues"

Triggerfish Critical Review – "Tell Them a Story"

The Write Helper – "If Love is a Big City, Lately I've Considered Relocating"

About the Author

Photo by Lowell Wagoner

Adrian S. Potter humbly lives in Minnesota on the traditional, ancestral, and contemporary lands of the Dakota people. When he's not busy silently judging your beer selection and record collection, he's talking too much or writing poetry and prose. His work has appeared in over 300 literary journals and magazines Potter is the author of three collections of poetry/prose/hybrid work, including *And the Monster Swallows You Whole* and *Field Guide to the Human Condition*. Visit him online at adrianspotter.com

About the Publisher

Escape the Mundane | Est. 2015

Follow us on:

Scan the QR code for www.thirtywestph.com